Music of the World
for
Mountain Dulcimer

by Neal He
and Janet H

Cover art by Shiloh Hellman

ISBN 978-1-4584-8269-3

HAL•LEONARD®
CORPORATION

7777 W. BLUEMOUND RD. P.O. BOX 13819 MILWAUKEE, WI 53213

In Australia Contact:
Hal Leonard Australia Pty. Ltd.
4 Lentara Court
Cheltenham, Victoria, 3192 Australia
Email: ausadmin@halleonard.com.au

Visit Hal Leonard Online at
www.halleonard.com

Contents

Acknowledgments

Special thanks to: Deby Benton Grosjean for help in editing the music; William Coulter, Kim Robertson, Verlene Schermer, Mary McLaughlin, Michael Strunk, and Peter Denee for helping us with the arrangements; Karen Mueller, Mark Gilston, Mark L. Nelson, and Paul Oorts for their arrangements; Victoria Smigelski for language assistance; Patricia Zylius for editing the text; Shiloh Hellman for the cover design and his help in our song quest; and Kevin Moore, our forever Finale guru.

About the CD

Singers: Janet Herman, Neal Hellman, Verlene Schermer, Mirian Song, Shelley Phillips, Debra Spencer, Vlada Volkova, and Mandy Spitzer.

Produced and engineered by Barry Phillips.

About the Songs

Before each song will be some notes about its origin and performance. There are countless versions of almost all the songs on YouTube. Keep in mind that they may not be in the same key or arrangement as in this book. All arrangements are in D–A–D tuning unless otherwise noted. Remember to listen to the accompanying CD, and don't forget to have fun!

Please note: The vocal version will vary from the dulcimer arrangement. Follow the chords!

Many of the arrangements in this book can be found on YouTube. You can find links to these at: *http://www.gourd.com/worldmusicdulcimerbook.html*

About the Notation and Tab

The songs in this book are notated in both standard notation and tablature. Most of the tunes also have back-up chord symbols written above the musical staff, with fret numbers next to the chord letters. Here is an example of the chord notation:

Gm 3 ⬅ bass string
0 ⬅ middle string
4 ⬅ unison or treble strings

This Gm chord is played with the treble strings fretted at the fourth fret and the bass string fretted at the third fret. More on dulcimer notation can be found in the *Hal Leonard Dulcimer Method*.

Please note: On a number of tunes, the rhythm and strumming on the accompanying CD differ from the notation in the tablature. For example, in the arrangement of "Asika Thali," though the vocal follows the written melody, the strumming differs in some places. In the opening pickup bar, the first 8th note is divided into two 16th notes. The beat is subdivided into additional strums to create more vitality in the performance. Subdivision of the beat also occurs in bar 2, where the first note (E) has been subdivided into an 8th note followed by two 16th notes. If you listen to the recording, you may hear other examples of this kind of rhythmic variation. Though the rhythmic structure is a little more complex, the basic melody has not been changed.

TRACK 1

TRACK 2
(Vocal)

Arirang

Trad. Korean
Arr. Neal Hellman

There are many versions of this popular Korean folk melody, whose roots go back over 600 years. My contribution is the F♯m chord in the 10th measure. I changed the timing in the sixth measure. It should be the same as measure 14, but I just wanted to add a little variation.

Alfonso X el Sabio

Trad. Spanish, 13th Century
Arr. Neal Hellman

Alfonso X "el Sabio" (the Wise) was King of Castille and Leon in 1252. One of his many contributions to music was his production of the *Cantigas de Santa María.*

The pull-off in measure 10 (7–6.5–4) might be a little tricky for some players. You could play the sixth fret of the middle string instead of the fourth fret of the treble string, as they are both a G note. Or you could simply strike the fourth fret of the treble string and not pull off from the 6.5 fret.

Tuning: CC-A-D

Moderately

Asika Thali

TRACK 4   TRACK 5
          (Vocal)

Trad. South African
Arr. Neal Hellman

You can play the first part of the melody of this South African folk song starting on the fourth fret of the treble string if you wish and then switch over to the middle string where indicated. Learn as written first, then try adding the extra strums as heard on the recording.

This song of freedom is translated:

The load is heavy; it requires the strength of men;
Even if we are arrested, we will get our freedom.

Tuning: DD-A-D

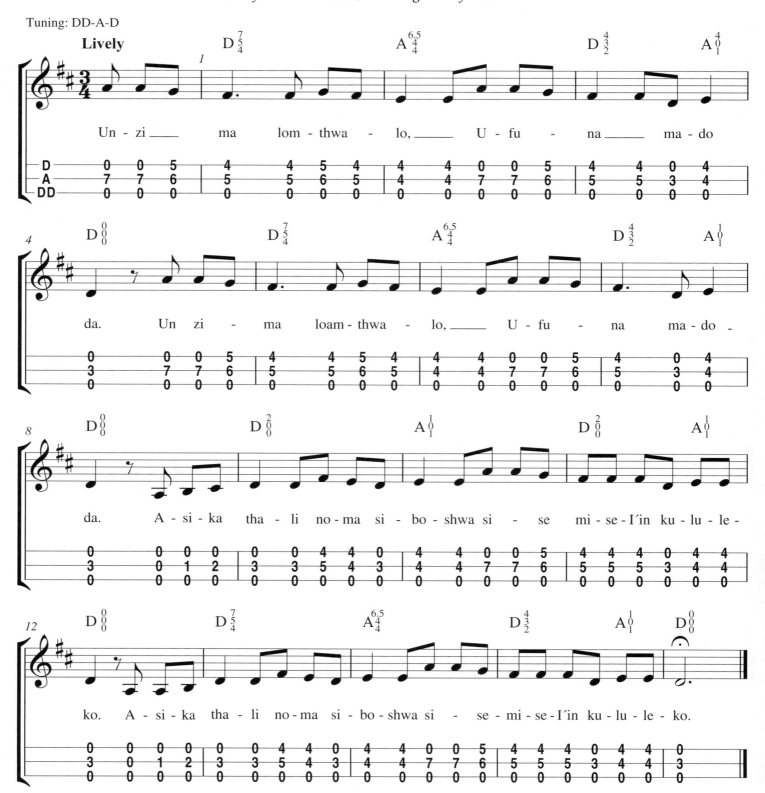

Bai, baï, baï, baï
(Two Versions)

Trad. Russian
Arr. Neal Hellman

This Russian lullaby is arranged for two different tunings. The first is in CC–A–D, and the second arrangement is in CC–G–C with a capo on fret 1. They are both very simple, but each one has its texture. Version 2 is translated in English.

Version 1

Tuning: CC-A-D

Baï, baï, baï, baï, baï-yu ___ dié-toch-kou ma-you.

Chto na gor-kié, na gar-ié po ves-en-ney o por-ié.
Ptitc-ki bo-je ye poy-out vtiom-nom lié-cie gnioz-da vyout.

Version 2

TRACK 7   TRACK 9
(Vocal)

Tuning: CC-G-C
Capo I

By, by, by, by, by you ___ walk-ing lit-tle deer.

On the hill-side in the spring, birds of heav-en sweet-ly sing.
Seek-ing for their young one's best, in the for-est dark they nest.

The Bamboo Flute

Trad. Chinese Lullaby from Shandong
Arr. Janet Herman

TRACK 10

Try to bring out this lovely melody on the high string as much as possible, as if you were playing a smooth, gentle musical line on the *erhu* (Chinese violin). The drone notes should be in the background. In the tab, the numbers in parentheses are just quiet filler notes and not part of the melody. (This is why you do not see them notated in the music staff.)

Tuning: DD-A-D

Moderately slow

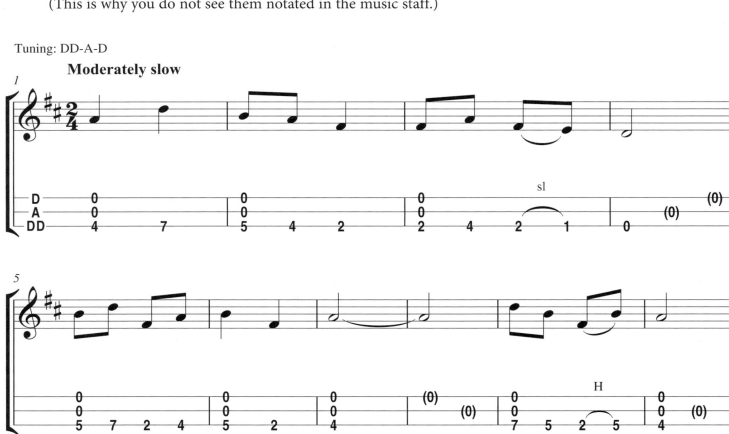

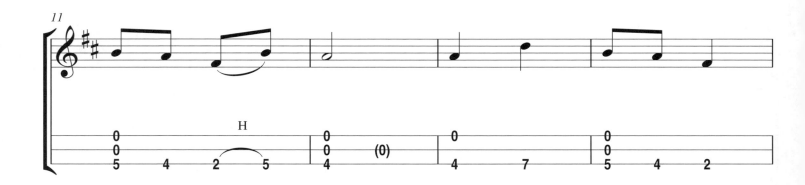

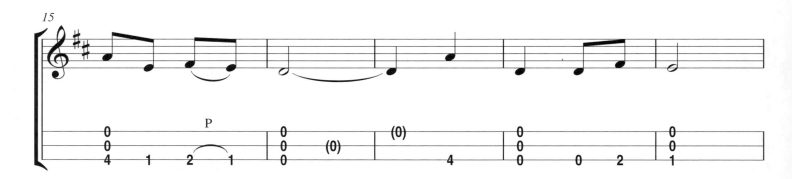

Belle qui tiens ma vie
(Beautiful One Who Holds My Life)

Thoinet Arbeau (1519–1595)
Arr. Neal Hellman

Thoinet Arbeau (1519–1595) was a Catholic priest who in 1588 published a very notable dance manuscript titled *Orchesography*.

Remember to capo on the fourth fret and tune DD–A–D. You don't have to employ a chord for each note, but I have found that it suits the feeling of this romantic 16th-century ballad.

Tuning: DD-A-D

Slow and Stately

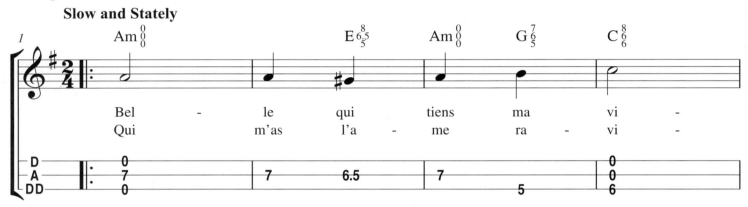

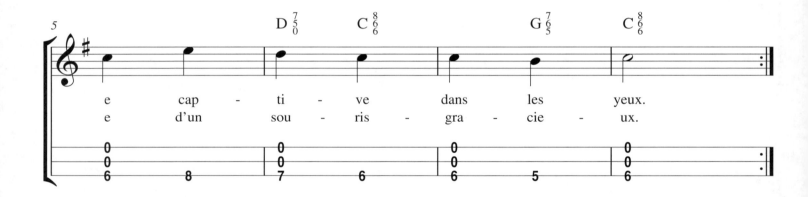

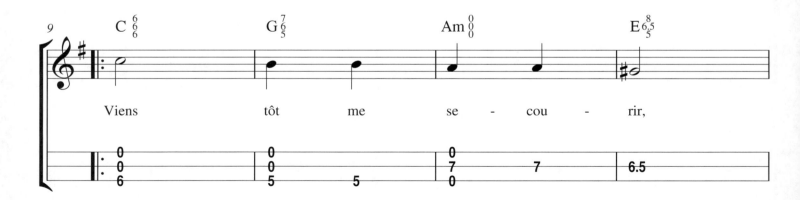

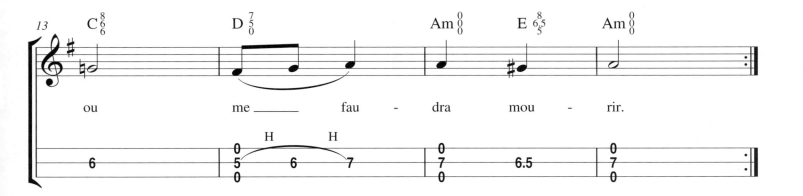

ou   me _____ fau - dra mou - rir.

Additional Lyrics

Belle qui tiens ma vie, captive dans tes yeux,
Qui m'as l'ame ravie, d'un sourire gracieux,
Viens tôt me secourir, Ou me faudra mourir,
Viens tôt me secourir, Ou me faudra mourir.

Pourquoi fuis tu, mignarde, si je suis pres de toi?
Quand tes yeux je regarde, je me perds dedans moi,
Car tes perfection, changent mes actions
Car tes perfection, changent mes actions.

Tes beautes et ta graces, et tes divins propos
Ont echauffe la glace, qui me gelait les os,
Et ont rempli mon Coeur, d'une amoureuse ardeur
Et ont rempli mon Coeur, d'une amoureuse ardeur.

Mon ame voulait etre, libre de passion,
Mais l'amour s'est fait maitre, de mes affections
Et a mis sous sa loi, et mon coeur et ma foi
Et a mis sous sa loi, et mon coeur et ma foi.

Approche donc ma belle, approche toi mon bien,
Ne me sois plus rebelled, puisque mon coeur est tien,
Pour mon mal appaiser, donne moi un baiser
Pour mon mal appaiser, donne moi un baiser.

Je meurs, mon Angelette, je meurs en te baisant
Ta bouche tant Doucette, va mon bien ravissant
A ce coup mes esprits, sont tous d'amour epris.

Plutot on verra l'onde, contremont reculer,
Et plutot l'oeil du monde, cessera de bruler,
Que l'amour qui m'epoint, decroisse d'un seul point
Que l'amour qui m'epoint, decroisse d'un seul point.

The Blackest Crow

Trad. American
Arr. Neal Hellman

TRACK 13   TRACK 14
                (Vocal)

If you'd like to just strum the whole tune, you need not play the embellishments.

Tuning: DD-A-D

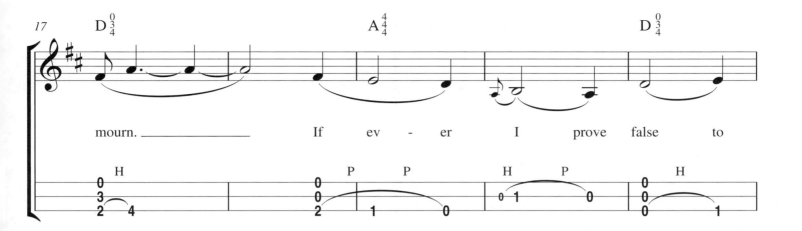

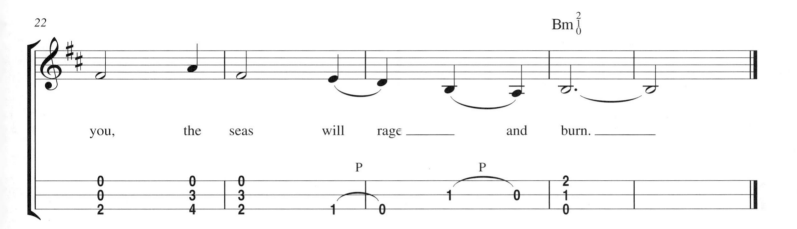

Additional Lyrics

I wish my heart was made of glass wherein you might behold
That there your name is written dear in letters made of gold.
In letters made of gold, my dear, believe me when I say
You are the only one for me until my dying day.

As time grows near, my dearest dear, when you and I must part
How little you know of the grief and woe in my poor aching heart.
'Tis but I'd suffer for your sake, believe me dear it's true
I wish that you were staying here or I was going with you.

Canarios

Gaspar Sanz (1640–1710)
Arr. Neal Hellman

This piece by Gaspar Sanz is probably one of the most difficult pieces I have arranged. I like to play it on my small dulcimer in the key of G. There are many versions of this composition; I learned this one (key of D) from the talented guitarist William Coulter.

Tuning: DD-A-D

Lively

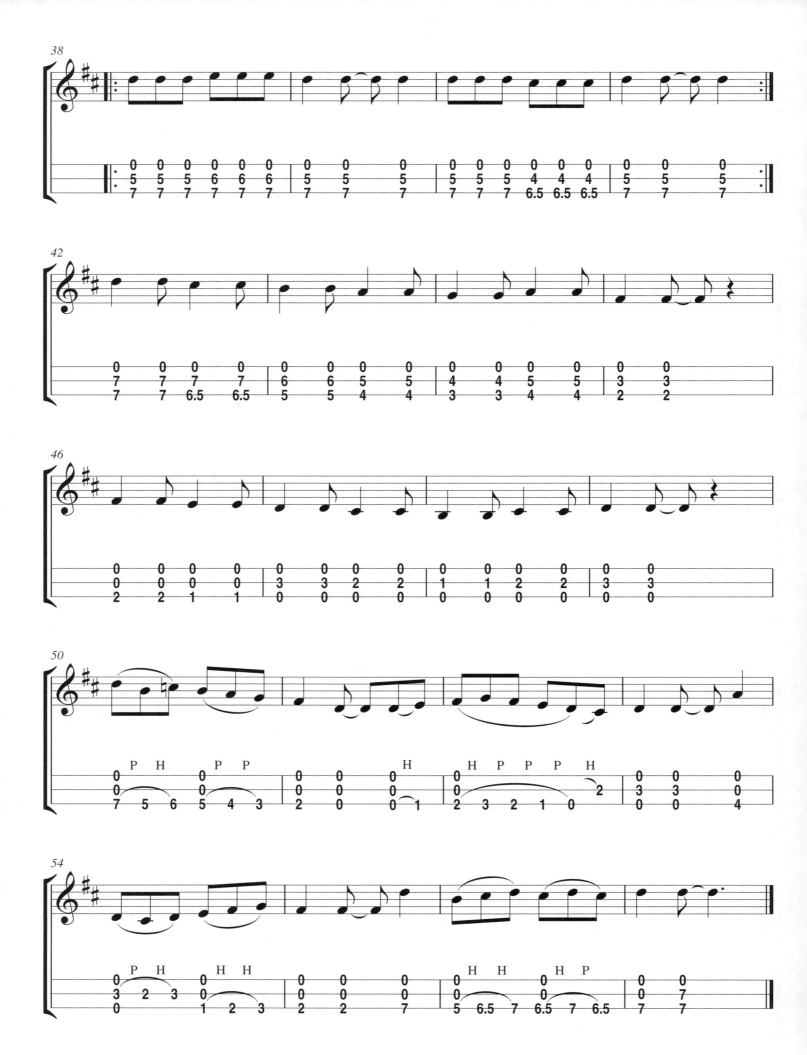

TRACK 16 TRACK 17
(Vocal)

C'est l'aviron quis nous mène en haut
(It Is the Oar That Impels Us On)

Trad. French Canadian
Arr. Neal Hellman

Tune to DD–G–D to play this French Canadian song about love and canoeing. Remember, since you are tuned to DD–G–D, you can play the melody on the bass string as well as the treble strings. I learned this one in Canada from Dan Bryant.

Tuning: DD-G-D

Spirited

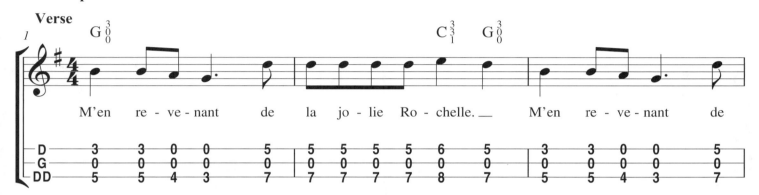

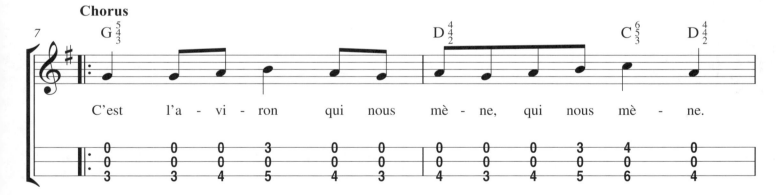

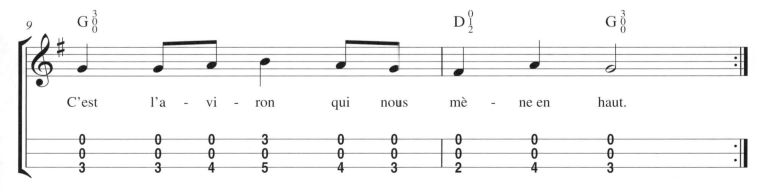

De colores

TRACK 18   TRACK 19
            (Vocal)

Trad. Mexican
Arr. Janet Herman

This traditional folk song is sung by Spanish speakers across the world. The arrangement here is designed for easy sliding up and down the fretboard, with a default position of ring finger on the high string and middle finger on the middle string. The index finger is sometimes called into action on the low string. An exception is measure 11, where the middle finger is on the low string and the thumb is on the high string. In several places where the vocal melody is tied over the bar line, you can repeat the dulcimer chord on the first beat of each measure to help mark time under the held vocal note.

Tuning: DD-A-D

Des oge mais

Trad. Galician-Portuguese Cantiga
Arr. Janet Herman

One of the songs found in *Cantigas de Santa Maria*, compiled under the reign of Castilian monarch Alfonso X "el Sabio" (1221–1284), "Des oge mais" lists the seven joys of Mary.

Default finger position is index finger on the low string, middle finger on the middle string, and thumb on the high string doing most of the fancy work. The ring finger also drops down on the melody string when necessary. For example, in measures 6–7, the thumb does all the slide work, then the ring finger plays the last note of measure 7. Also use the thumb for slide work on the middle string in passages such as that in measure 30.

Tuning: DD-A-D

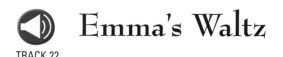

Emma's Waltz

Trad. Finnish
Arr. Neal Hellman

TRACK 22

For this traditional Finnish waltz, tune DD–A–D and capo the first fret. To play the phrase in measure 28, you will probably have to slide (sl) from the fifth to the sixth fret.

Tuning: DD-A-D
Capo I

Spirited

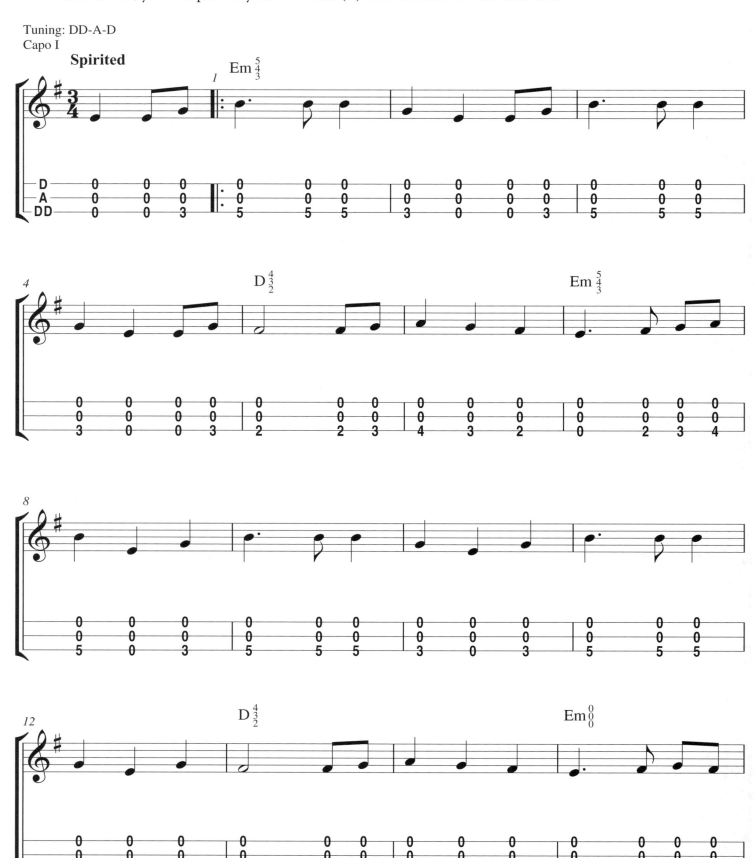

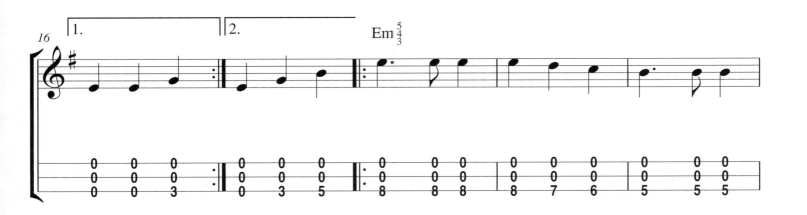

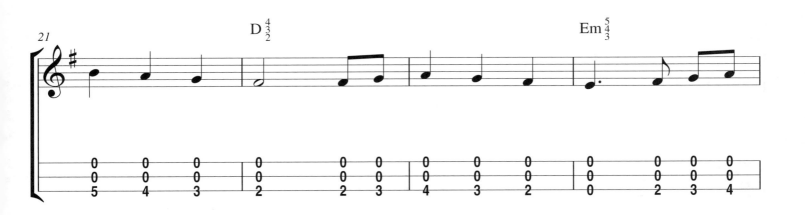

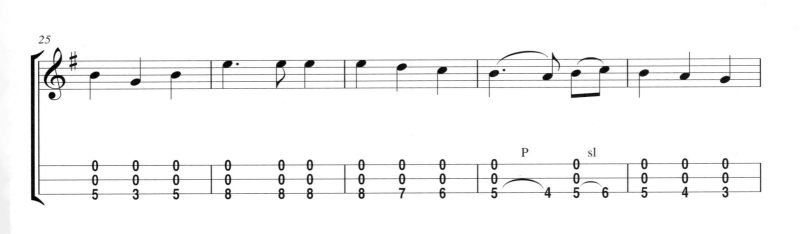

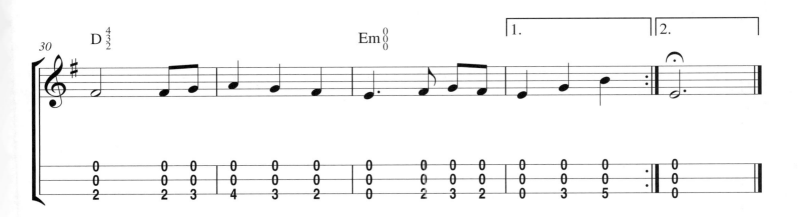

Do'n Oíche Úd i mBeithil
(To That Night Long Ago in Bethlehem)

Irish Christmas Carol
Arr. Neal Hellman

The top line of the lyrics is the phonetics, and the line under that is Irish. The phonetic arrangement is by Mary McLaughlin, from her recording *A Gaelic Christmas*.

Tuning: DD-A-D

Moderately slow

Hine ma tov
(Behold How Good)

Trad. Israeli
Arr. Janet Herman

Tune DD-A-D and capo on the fifth fret. This traditional two-part round in Hebrew is from Psalm 133: "Behold how good and how pleasant it is for humankind to live together in unity."

When six 8th notes are found in a row, use the strum pattern "down-up-down, down-up-down." For the vocal version, the arrangement is performed several times with vocals singing in a round.

Tuning: DD-A-D
Capo V

Moderately

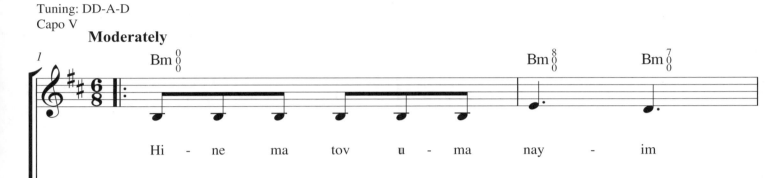

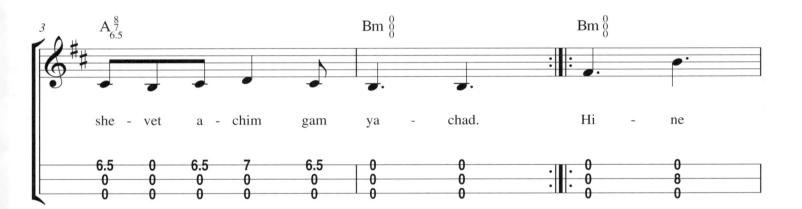

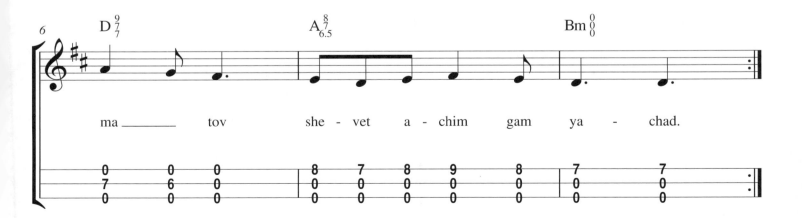

I Will Arise

TRACK 27   TRACK 28
(Vocal)

Trad. American
Arr. Neal Hellman

This is one of my favorite hymns. This *pentatonic* (five-note) melody is also found in *The Sacred Harp* tune book, where it is known as "Come Thou Fount of Every Blessing."

Tuning: DD-A-D

Slowly

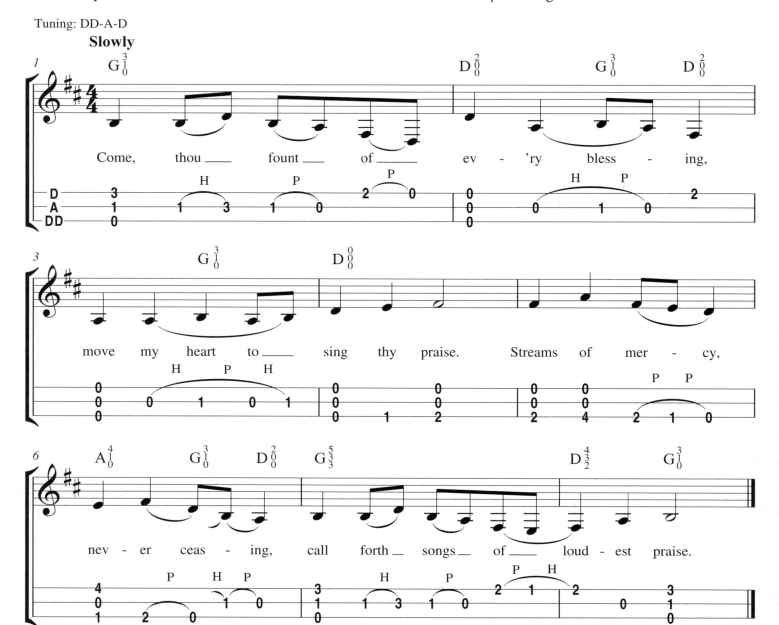

Additional Lyrics

I will arise and go to Jesus;
He will embrace me in his arms.
In the arms of my dear Savior,
Oh, there are ten thousand charms.

Teach me some melodious songs,
Sung by flaming tongues above.
Here's the Mount; I'm fixed upon it
Songs of Thy redeeming love.

Here I'll raise my songs in praise;
Hither, by Thy help, I'm bound.
And I pray, by Thy good pleasure,
Safely to arrive at home.

TRACK 29 TRACK 30
(Vocal)

If I Was a Blackbird

Trad. Scottish
Arr. Neal Hellman

I learned this beautiful Scottish ballad from the singing of the group Silly Wizard. Start the tune with your thumb on the second fret of the melody string, your middle finger on the first fret of the middle string, index finger on the second fret of the bass string, and your ring finger on the first fret of the melody string.

Tuning: DD-A-D

Moderately

I _____ am a _____ young sail - or; my sto - ry is _____ sad. Oh once I was care - free and a brave sail - or lad. I _____ court - ed a lass - ie by night and by day. Ah, but now she's _____ left me here and sailed _____ far a - way.

Kalendara

Trad. Croatian
Arr. Mark Gilston

Throughout northern Croatia and parts of Serbia and Hungary, a great deal of traditional music is played on a mandolin-like instrument called a *tamburitza*. Tamburitzas are played in bands with instruments of different sizes taking the roles of melody, harmony, rhythmic chords, and bass.

The most common dance tunes of the region are called *kolos* (circle dances) and are generally danced in rings or by couples and typified by a continuous, small bouncing motion. Kolo melodies tend to be relatively short, simple tunes that are repeated and played in several related keys. When playing kolos, one should adapt a rhythmic, almost tremolo-like strum on the sustained pitches, giving the piece a staccato feel.

The 8–4–4 and 7–3–3 chords are basic barre chords. I recommend playing them with the thumb on frets 8 and 7, respectively, and the ring and middle fingers for the –4–4 and the –3–3. When I play them, my pinky also remains firmly on the fourth/third fret on the melody string. When playing barre chords, use the pinky, ring, and middle fingers, with the thumb as a sort of a surrogate "noter" for playing melody above the barre.

This arrangement is by Mark Gilston. You can see Mark playing "Kalendara" at *http://www.gourd.com/worldmusicdulcimerbook.html*.

Tuning: DD-A-D

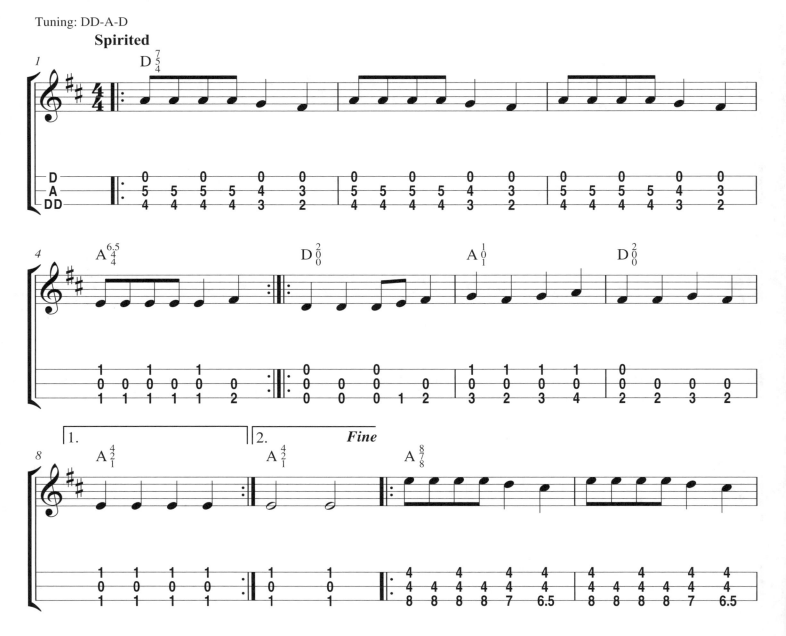

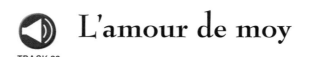

L'amour de moy

TRACK 32

Anon. French, 15th Century
Arr. Neal Hellman

This beautiful French love song is from the 15th-century collection of music *Le manuscript de Bayeux*. This instrumental version was inspired by Charlie Haden and Hank Jones from their wonderful recording *Steal Away: Spirituals, Hymns and Folk Songs* (Verve Records, 1995).

Tuning: DD-A-D

Moderately slow

Kōjō no tsuki

(Moon Over the Ruined Castle)

Rentarō Taki (1879–1903)
Arr. Neal Hellman

Tune CC–A–D to play this classic Japanese melody, written by Rentarō Taki (1879–1903). The ruins of Oka Castle, built in 1185, inspired Taki. Little did he know his enchanting melody would be recorded many times by various musicians, from Thelonious Monk to the German metal band Scorpions.

Tuning: CC-A-D

Slowly

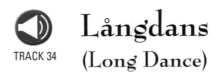

Långdans
(Long Dance)

Trad. Swedish
From the playing of Roger Tallroth

Here is a very simple and pleasurable exercise in hammer-ons and pull-offs, from the playing of
Roger Tallroth of the Swedish group Väsen.

Tuning: DD-A-D

The Last Time I Came O'er the Moor

Traditional Scottish (Thumoth collection, 1748)
Arr. Neal Hellman

This was originally a Scottish air that Robert Burns later used in 1793 for a very sad love song. It's from the recording *Jefferson's Fiddle* by William Coulter and Deby Benton Grosjean.

Tuning: DD-A-D

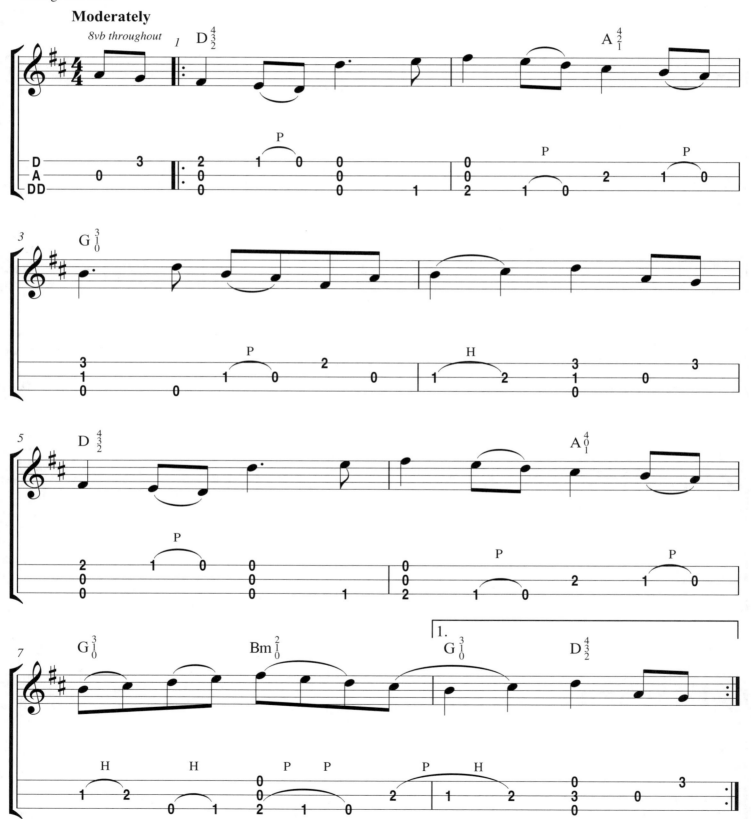

Lauda di Maria Maddalenna

Italian Lauda (12th century)
Arr. Neal Hellman

This is a 12th-century Italian song of praise (*lauda*) from Florence. In measures 14, 15, 17, and 18, try picking through the individual notes of the chords. You can listen to another vocal version of it here: *http://www.gourd.com/worldmusicdulcimerbook.html*

Tuning: DD-A-D

Slowly

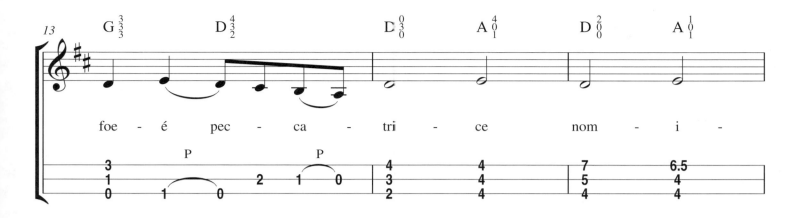

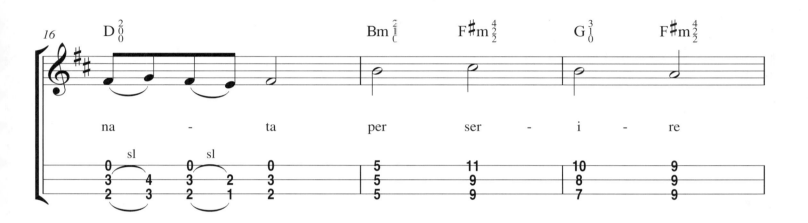

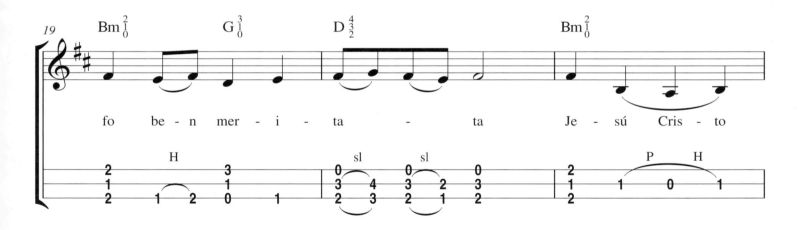

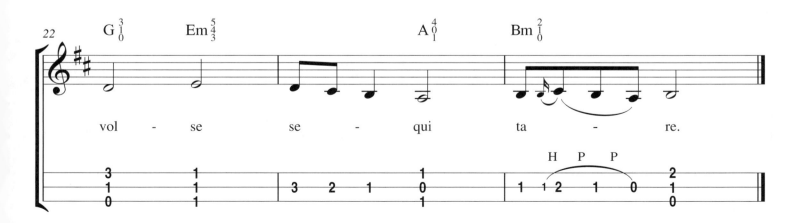

TRACK 38 TRACK 39
(Vocal)

Lördagsvisa
(Saturday Song)

Trad. Swedish
Arr. Neal Hellman

To play that tricky 2–1–3 chord (3 is the bass), I use my middle finger on the second fret of the treble string, ring finger on the first fret of the middle string, and index finger on the third fret of the bass string. I learned this Swedish song from the playing of Verlene Schermer, who performs it on the nyckelharpa.

Tuning: DD-A-D

Moderately

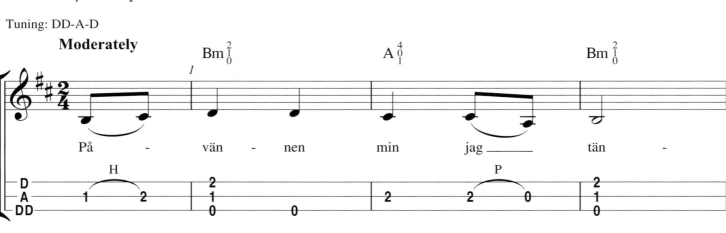

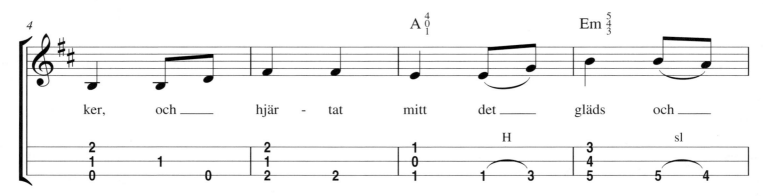

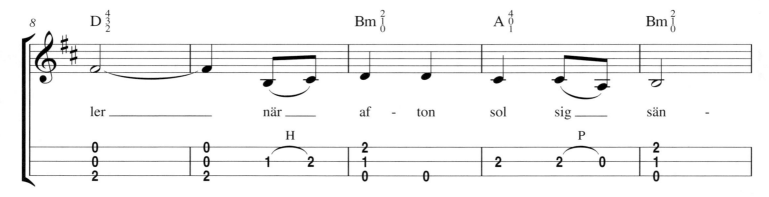

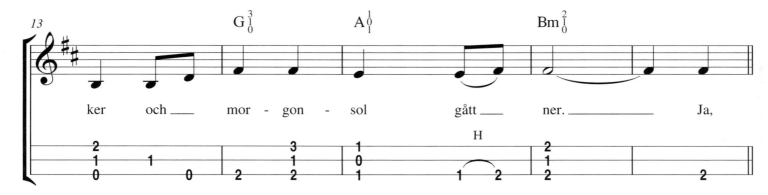

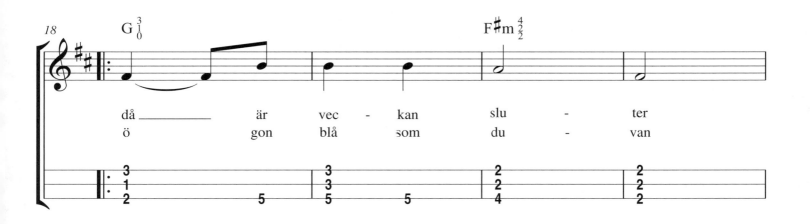

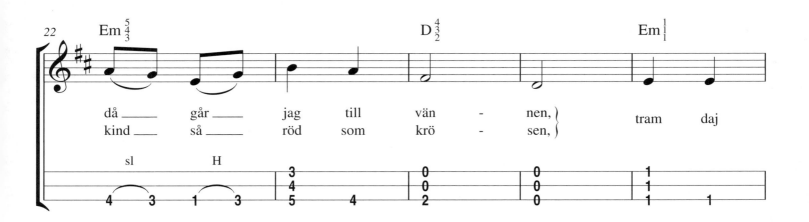

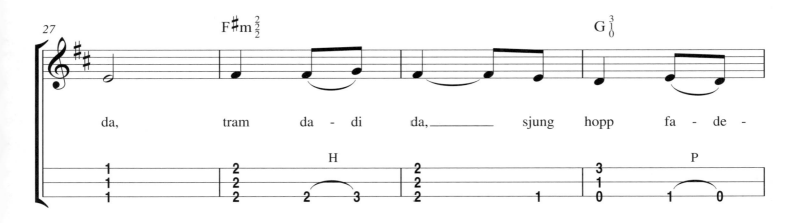

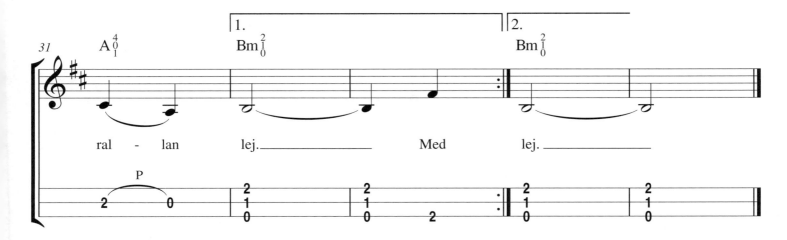

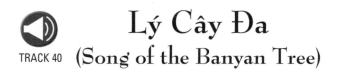

Lý Cây Đa
(Song of the Banyan Tree)

TRACK 40

Trad. Vietnamese
Arr. Karen Mueller

This well-known traditional Vietnamese folk song may be heard in a variety of musical settings, from the traditional Phong Nguyen Ensemble arrangement to a pop version by singer Ho Ngoc Ha. The tempo is lively (175 bpm), but it also sounds sweet and lyrical at slower speeds. This finger-picked arrangement allows for simple fills on the longer notes, with hammer-ons and pull-offs to smooth out the melody.

Tuning: DD-A-D

Moderately fast

Menuet 70 de Gruijtters

Johannes de Gruijtters (1709–1772)
Belgium
Arr. Paul Oorts

Johannes de Gruijtters (1709–1772) won the competition for the position of city carilloneur at the Cathedral of Our Lady (Onze Lieve Vrouwekathedraal) in the city of Antwerp in 1740. The cathedral had a unique attribute: its tower contained two complete carillons. One was known as the "kapittelbeiaard;" it belonged to the church and was supposed to be used for playing religious music for processions, etc. The other, called "kermisbeiaard," belonged to the city and performed secular music for festive public occasions. In 1746, Johannes compiled, for his own private use, a handwritten collection of 194 pieces arranged for the carillon, mostly secular in nature. Almost half of them are minuets, which testifies to the great popularity of that dance form in the mid-1700s.

Tuning: DD-A-D

Moderately

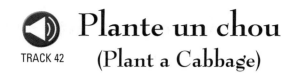

Plante un chou
(Plant a Cabbage)

Trad. French
Arr. Janet Herman

Here is one of many fun, upbeat bagpipe and hurdy gurdy dance tunes from central France. This arrangement evokes the drone strings and circular phrasing of the hurdy gurdy. It requires a lot of quick thumb action. For example, in measure 12, the thumb dances up the middle string, then moves to the high string while the index and middle fingers remain anchored in place on the low and middle strings, respectively (but use the ring finger on the high string for the 1–1–2 chord). Alternate up and down strums for passages of 16th notes.

Tuning: DD-A-D

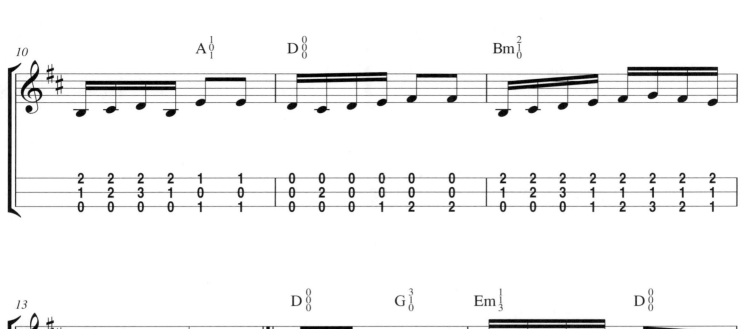

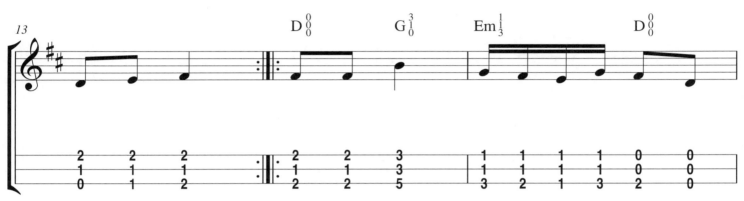

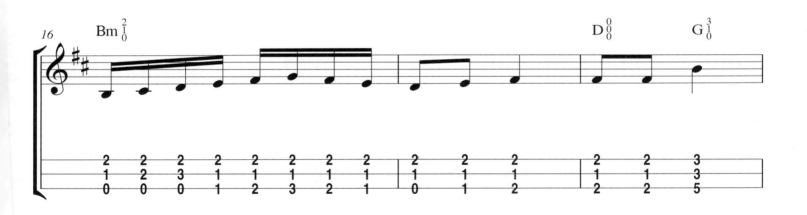

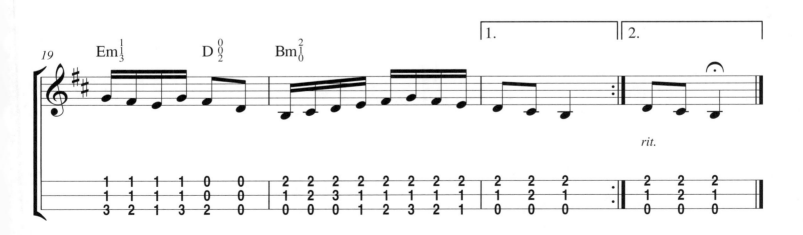

TRACK 43   TRACK 44
(Vocal)

Ojos azules
(Blue Eyes)

Trad. Andean
Arr. Neal Hellman

Tune DD–A–D and place your capo on the fourth fret. You can play this sad Andean ballad all on the melody string without any chords at all. However, you will need to strike the sixth fret of the middle string (G) in the measure 7.

Listen online at *http://www.gourd.com/worldmusicdulcimerbook.html*

Tuning: DD-A-D
Capo IV

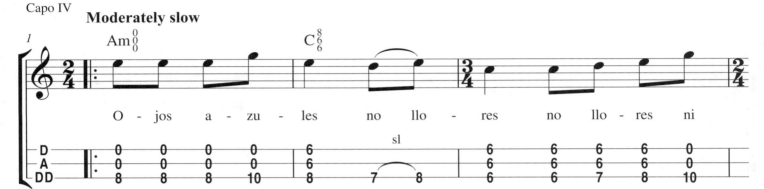

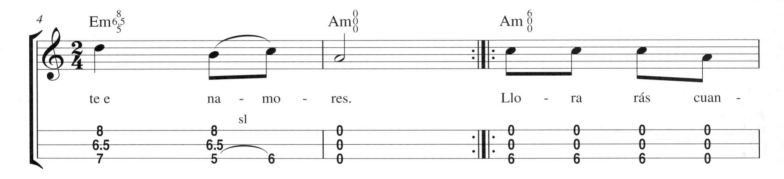

Additional Lyrics

Tú me juraste quererme,
Quererme toda la vida.
Tú me juraste quererme,
Quererme toda la vida.
No han pasado dos, tres días
Tú te alejas y me dejas.
No han pasado dos, tres días
Tú te alejas y me dejas.

En una copa de vino
Quisiera tomar veneno.
En una copa de vino
Quisiera tomar veneno.
Veneno para matarme
Veneno para olvidarte.
Veneno para matarme
Veneno para olvidarte.

Roselil' og hendes moder
(Rosie and Her Mother)

Trad. Danish
Arr. Neal Hellman

This fun Danish waltz was simply made for the dulcimer. Try adding a pause after you play the A chord in measure 16.

Tuning: DD-A-D

Moderately fast

Säckpiplåt e. Carl Wahlström

Trad. Swedish
Arr. Neal Hellman

"Säckpiplåt" is a Swedish bagpipe tune from Northern Värmland. This one is challenging, and it's best to take it measure by measure. I learned this version from Shelley Phillips' recording, *The Butterfly.* Tune to CC–A–D.

Tuning: CC-A-D

Moderately

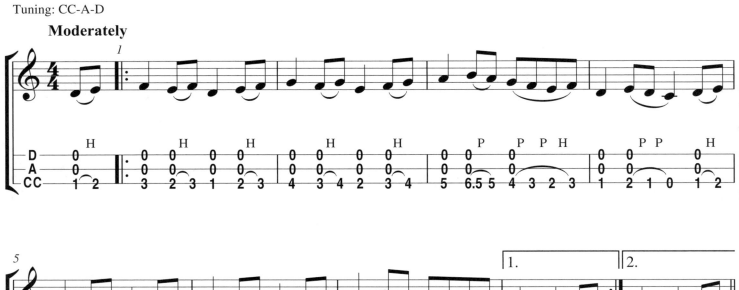

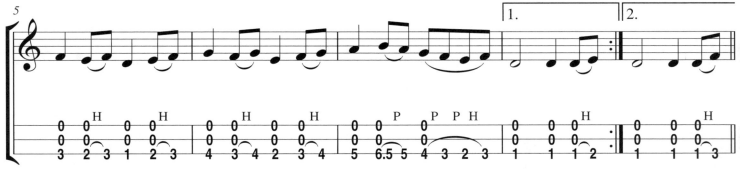

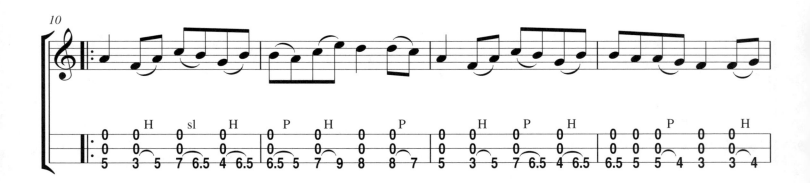

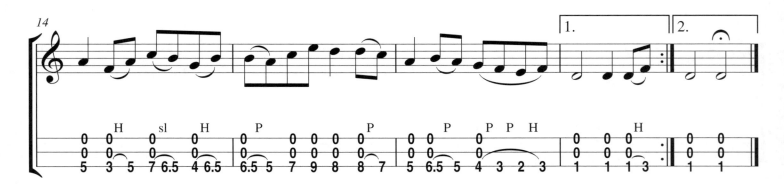

Saltarello

Italian
Vincenzo Galilei (1520–1591)
Arr. Neal Hellman

TRACK 47

"Saltarello" was written by Vincenzo Galilei, the father of Galileo. Play this one slowly until you get comfortable with all the embellishments and the feel of the piece. Celtic harper extraordinaire Kim Robertson taught me this Italian dance melody.

Tuning: DD-A-D

TRACK 48 TRACK 49
(Vocal)

Slumber My Darling

Stephen Foster (1826–1864)
Arr. Neal Hellman

This is the arrangement I played with Kim Robertson on her recording, *Shady Grove*. If the 4–2–1 chord is too much of a stretch, you could get away with 4–4–4.

Note that the vocal version has some extra beats on held notes and in between stanzas.

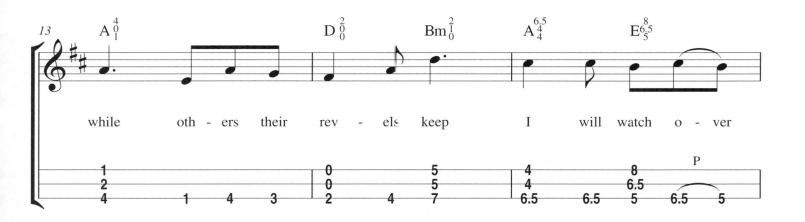

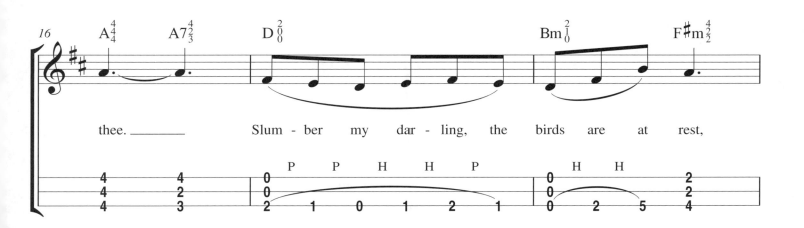

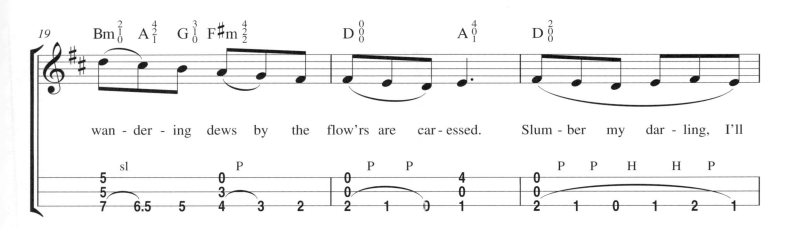

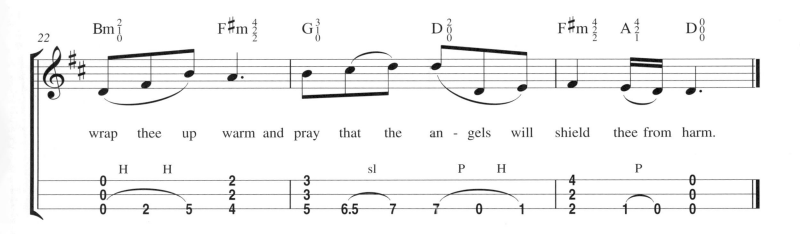

Additional Lyrics

Slumber, my darling, thy mother is near,
Guarding thy dreams from all terror and fear.
Sunlight has pass'd, and the twilight has gone,
Slumber, my darling, the night's coming on.
Sweet visions attend thy sleep,
Fondest, dearest to me,
While others their revels keep,
I will watch over thee.
Slumber, my darling, the birds are at rest,
Wandering dews by the flow'rs are caressed.
Slumber, my darling, I'll wrap thee up warm
And pray that the angels will shield thee from harm.

Slumber, my darling, till morn's blushing ray
Brings to the world the glad tidings of day;
Fill the dark void with thy dreamy delight
Slumber, thy mother will guard thee tonight.
Thy pillow shall sacred be
From all outward alarms;
Thou, thou are the world to me
In thine innocent charms.
Slumber, my darling, the birds are at rest,
Wandering dews by the flow'rs are caressed.
Slumber, my darling, I'll wrap thee up warm
And pray that the angels will shield thee from harm.

TRACK 50   TRACK 51
              (Vocal)

Shto mi e milo

Trad. Macedonian
Arr. Janet Herman

A very popular folk dance tune in Eastern European dance circles in the United States, this song is about a young man who would like to have a shop in Struga to watch the girls go by. This arrangement can be flatpicked or fingerpicked, but I find fingerpicking is easier to control. The hardest part is the 7/8 meter. Each measure has a long beat followed by two short beats. They can be counted "one–two–three, one–two, one–two."

On the audio, the vocal version runs through the full arrangement twice.

Tuning: DD-A-D

Srpkinja
(Serbian Girl)

Trad. Serbian
Arr. Mark Gilston

This is a Serbian *kolo*, which is danced by couples in a circle. Couple dances are very unusual in Serbia, though they are quite common in Croatia and Hungary. When playing kolos, one should adapt a short, rhythmic strumming on the sustained pitches, giving the piece a staccato feel. To maintain this strong rhythmic feeling, I have inserted some rhythmic fills and riffs that are not part of the melody proper. These are designated by small notes in parentheses and give the piece the typical feel of a tamburitza band. You can see Mark Gilston playing his arrangement of "Srpkinja" at *http://www.gourd.com/worldmusicdulcimerbook.html.*

Tuning: DD-A-D

Studenten March

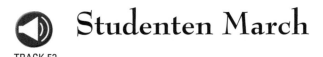

Trad. Netherlandish
Arr. Neal Hellman

This traditional tune from the Netherlands is a bit tricky. However, the good part is that you can play it slowly and stately. There are parts of the piece where I couldn't decide which embellishment to use. If employing a pull-off rather than a slide feels better for you, by all means do it.

Tuning: DD-A-D

Moderate and Stately

Sumer Is Icumen In

Trad. English Round (ca. 1310)
Arr. Neal Hellman

TRACK 54 TRACK 55
(Vocal)

This traditional round from England has been called the oldest written piece of six-part polyphonic music.

To perform this as a round, start with accompaniment #1 two times; then accompaniment #2 enters. The accompaniments continue throughout the entire piece. The first player begins the melody (1). When the first player arrives at measure 3, the second player begins the melody from the top. If you wish, you can add another melody at the fifth measure and one more at the seventh. The lyrics, in Middle English, celebrate the arrival of summer with its warm weather, when all nature rejoices. (On the second line of the lyrics, I have taken the liberty to translate some key words for those folks whose Middle English might be a little rusty.)

Tuning: DD-A-D

Joyful and Spirited

Melody

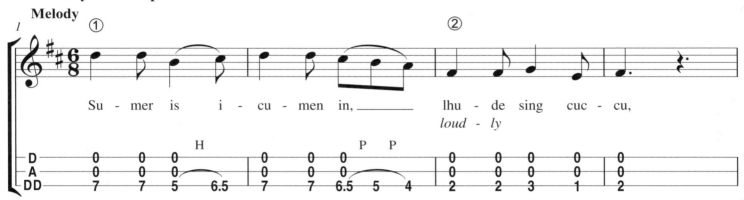

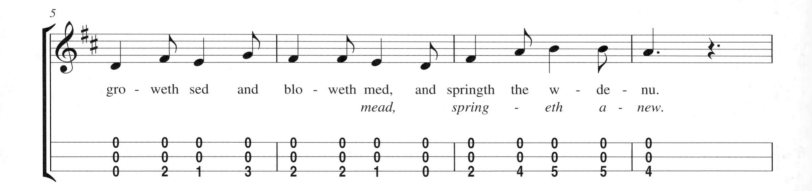

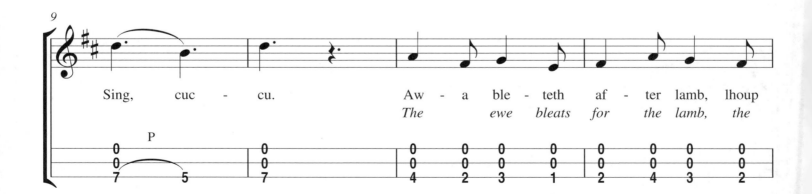

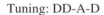

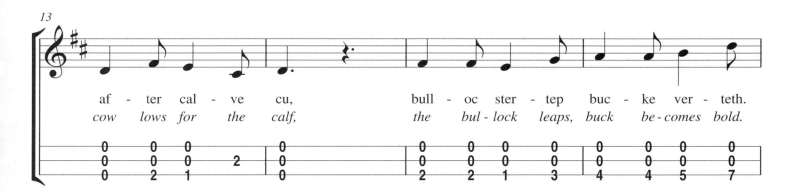

af - ter cal - ve cu, bull - oc ster - tep buc - ke ver - teth.
cow lows for the calf, the bul - lock leaps, buck be - comes bold.

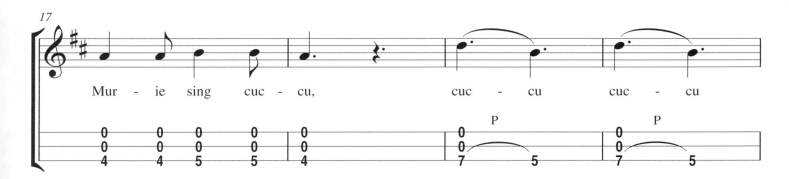

Mur - ie sing cuc - cu, cuc - cu cuc - cu

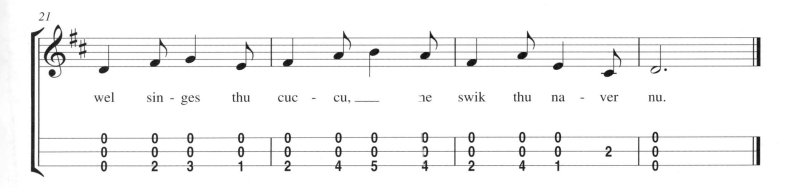

wel sin - ges thu cuc - cu, ____ ne swik thu na - ver nu.

Accompaniment 1

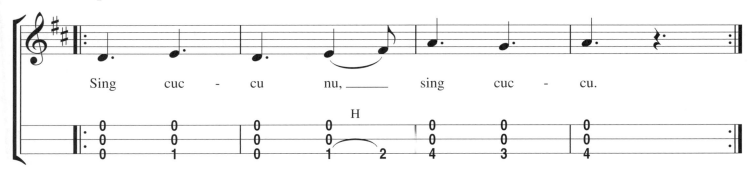

Sing cuc - cu nu, ____ sing cuc - cu.

Accompaniment 2

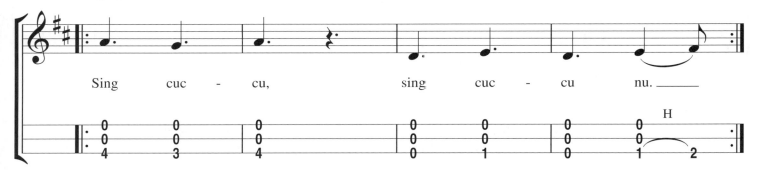

Sing cuc - cu, sing cuc - cu nu. ____

Tiare Tahiti

TRACK 56

Trad. Tahitian
Arr. Mark L. Nelson

The *tiare* is the Tahitian gardenia. It is said that once you smell its enticing fragrance, your thoughts will ever be on returning to this enchanted isle.

Tune CC–G–C. Fingerpick only the notes indicated and strive for a smooth flow between all the notes. The harmonics (called "chimes" in Hawaii), hammer-ons, pull-offs, and slides are typical of the slack-key style. Be sure to give each slurred note its full value. As with many slack-key arrangements, this arrangement includes an introduction to set the tone. The melody starts at measure 5 and is followed by a bridge section in a more modern style. After you play measures 19–22 twice, go back to measure 5 and play the song again.

Tuning: CC-G-C

Moderately

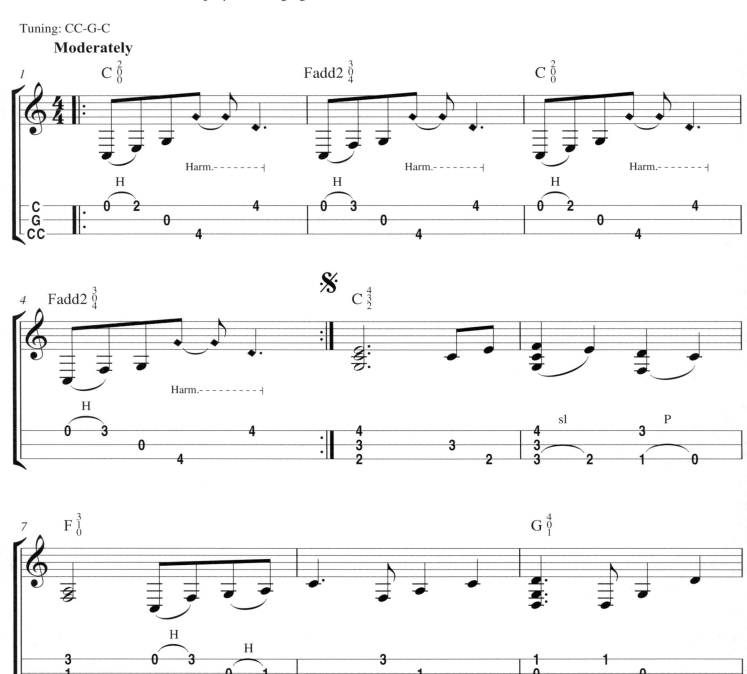

Tourdion

TRACK 57   TRACK 58
(Vocal)

Pierre Attaignant (1494–1551)
Arr. Neal Hellman

Tune CC–A–D to play this exciting song about the consumption of wine, written by French musician and music publisher Pierre Attaignant (1494–1551).

Start with your ring finger on the first fret and your middle and index fingers directly over the second and third frets, respectively. Then slide the assembly up one fret so you have your index finger on the fourth fret and your middle and ring fingers hovering over the third and second frets, respectively.

Listen to a very exciting version of "Tourdion" by the Moldavian group Ann'Sannat. It's also in Dm but just a shade different. Remember to sing along. *http://www.gourd.com/worldmusicdulcimerbook.html*

Tuning: CC-A-D

Moderately fast

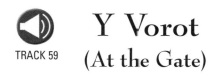

Y Vorot
(At the Gate)

Trad. Russian
Arr. Neal Hellman

Tune DD–A–D and capo on the first fret.

This lovely Russian dance is featured in Tchaikovsky's *1812 Overture*. Aleksander Ivanov-Kramskoi wrote variations on this melody. *http://www.gourd.com/worldmusicdulcimerbook.html*

Tuning: DD-A-D
Capo I

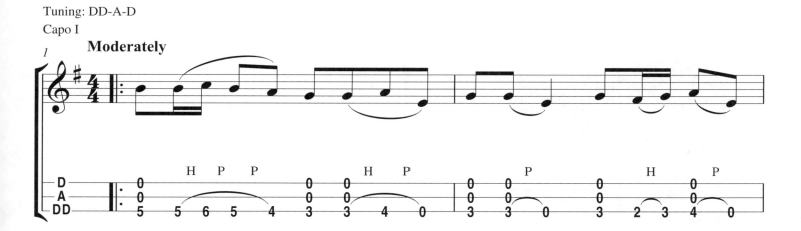

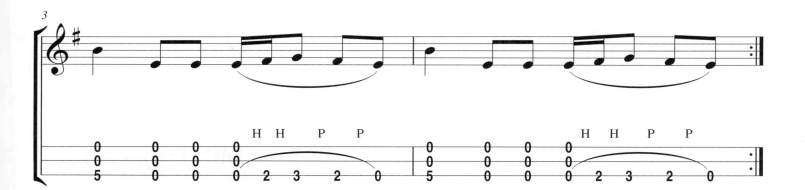

About the Authors

Neal Hellman

Neal Hellman, nationally acclaimed performer and teacher of the mountain dulcimer, has been active in performing, writing, teaching, and recording acoustic music for the past three decades. Neal's latest recording, *Emma's Waltz*, is a colorful dance through traditional and contemporary acoustic music styles. His other recordings include *Autumn in the Valley, Dream of the Manatee* (with Joe Weed), and *Oktober County*.

In collaboration with Joe Weed, Neal wrote the score for *Princess Furball*, a children's video by Weston Woods that won a 1993 American Library Association Commendation.

An original composition, written by Neal and performed by Jay Unger and Molly Mason, is featured on the Ken Burns production *Not for Ourselves Alone,* which was broadcasted on PBS nationwide in the fall of 1999.

Neal has written arrangement and method books for Mel Bay, the Richmond Organization, and Hal Leonard Corporation. His books include *Celtic Songs & Slow Airs for Mountain Dulcimer, The Dulcimer Chord Book, The Hal Leonard Dulcimer Method, Hits of the Beatles for Mountain Dulcimer,* and *The Music of the Shakers for Mountain Dulcimer.*

As founder, director, and one of the primary artists of the Gourd Music record label, Neal has produced over 40 recordings, including *Simple Gifts, Tree of Life, Pavane, Tender Shepherd, The World Turned Upside Down,* and *Jefferson's Fiddle.* Gourd Music specializes in a uniquely distinctive sound, featuring a variety of acoustic instrumental ensembles rich in texture and tonal color. In 2009, Neal served as the music director for a production of *The Grapes of Wrath*, which played at the Crocker Theater at Cabrillo College.

Janet Herman

Janet Herman has been playing and arranging music for dulcimer since her teen years in Los Angeles and has a musical background of unusual depth and breadth. She co-founded northern California's premiere mountain dulcimer retreat, Redwood Dulcimer Day, in 2001 and served as event director and on the teaching staff for its first ten years.

A lovely singer, she has been featured on Neal Hellman's *Hal Leonard Dulcimer Method* CD tutorial and releases by Zambra, a female world music vocal group, among other recordings. Janet studied early music at UC Riverside and then went on to earn a Ph.D. in Folklore/Ethno-musicology from UCLA, where she wrote a dissertation on Sacred Harp singing and played in a Balinese gamelan and a bluegrass band. Currently she loves Irish music, playing traditional tunes on tenor banjo, mandolin, and whistle, and also singing in Irish Gaelic. Additionally, Janet helps to preserve Himalayan folk music as the co-founder, writer, and research adviser for the Music of Bhutan Research Centre based in Thimphu, Bhutan.